Jennifer Walter

Australian Shepherd Grooming

Guide

All information in this book was conducted with greatest care. The author does not assume liability of personal injury or material damage which may be caused by practicing the shown methods and/or using the displayed materials. All prices and products were researched at the release of this book and may become obsolete.

This book is copyrighted. Publication or commercial use including excerpts have to be permitted by the author in writing.

Jennifer Walter

Am Ehrenmal 14

41564 Kaarst

Germany

Every commercial use of this text (e.g. its distribution as an audio file) or distribution of the text on websites or CDs without the author's written consent is prohibited.

© 2015 Jennifer Walter (info@yellowstoneaussies.de)

Translated and edited by Anna Bergenthal

All mentioned brand names are property of the respective companies. The brand names are used for informational purposes only.

Table of Contents

Introduction 5
- *Why Groom?* 6
- *When Should You Groom?* 7

Which Tools Do You Need? 8
- *Which Brushes Do You Need?* 8
- *Which Scissors Do You Need?* 9
- *How To Cut The Claws?* 10
- *Shampoos & Styling Products* 11
- *How To Dry Your Dog?* 13

Daily Grooming - A Pictured Guide 15
- *Brushing the body* 15
- *Brushing The Ears* 15
- *Brushing The Toby Collar* 15
- *Brushing The Paws* 16
- *Brushing The Britches* 16
- *Brushing The Tail* 17
- *Positive Reinforcement* 17

Cutting The Claws 18
- *Claw Cutting Guide* 18
- *Positive Reinforcement* 19

Show Grooming - A Pictured Guide 20
- *Removing The Fur Under The Paws* 20
- *Removing The Fur on The Paws* 21
- *Cutting The Fur on The Back of The Front Paws* ... 22
- *Grooming Hind Paws* 23
- *Grooming The Hocks* 24
- *Grooming The Ears* 26

Summary 28

Introduction

Because I am an Australian Shepherd breeder, I set my wits to dog shows and I learned how to present dogs from their best side. Several times a year, I prepare my dogs for showing.

Since it is hard to find information for newbies and interested people and because I wanted to have a handout for my stud dog owners, I wrote this book.

Our Yellowstone Pack Josie, Maisy, Layla & Seven

Some of the products and tools mentioned in this book may only be available on the German market. However, all mentioned URLs refer to Amazon.com. If you are interested in one of the mentioned items, just try to find the same or a similar item on e.g. the internet or ask at a pet store. Most vendors on Amazon.de also ship to locations outside Germany.

First of all, I will explain what grooming actually means. Next, I will comment on why grooming makes sense - also for pet dogs. After that, I will show you all the brushes and tools you will need. Finally, I will show you with a lot of photos - thanks to my bitch Josie for her perfect modelling job - each step you need to follow to improve the optics of your dog.

I wish you a lot of fun reading this book, watching the photos, and I hope that you and your dog enjoy grooming.

The author & some of her dogs Layla, Maisy & Josie

What is Grooming?

Grooming means to dress up, to prepare. In dog care, it means to tend, brush, comb the dog's fur and prepare it for showing.

In behavioural biology, grooming is part of comfort behaviour and indicates the personal hygiene of animals among themselves. So, grooming is not only the preparation for a dog show, it also strengthens the relationship between you and your dog. It is very important that all steps take place in a calm atmosphere and that the dog will be praised for its calm behaviour so that the relationship between you and your dog intensifies and so that both involved parties have fun.

Why Groom?

When we crazy Aussie fans hear the word "grooming", we immediately think about the styled poodles that proudly take the stage on glamorous shows. This kind of grooming has nothing to do with Aussie grooming – really NOTHING.

The Australian Shepherd is a working dog – a herding dog and it should be presented as such on shows. Aussies should be presented working, but they should impress the jury and the audience with a well-groomed and clean coat doing so. With the help of grooming, you can highlight your dog's charms and advantages. The breed standard stipulates:

> „*The coat is of medium length and texture, straight to slightly wavy, and weather resistant.*
>
> *The undercoat varies in quantity with climate. Hair is short and smooth on the head, outside of ears, front of forelegs, and below the hocks. Backs of forelegs are moderately feathered and breeches are moderately full.*
>
> *There is a moderate mane, more pronounced in dogs than bitches. The Australian Shepherd is a working dog and is to be shown with a natural coat.*
>
> *Severe Faults: Non-typical coats such as excessively long; overabundant/profuse; wiry; or curly.*"

Grooming does not only make sense for shows, also family dogs can benefit from styling. Removing the fur under and on the paws can prevent mud under the paws which can handicap the dog when working. Sometimes during winter, water can freeze under the paw and can lead to frostbites.

Most Aussies live with us in our homes, so when their paws are well-groomed, they will not carry as much mud inside. A lot of Aussies have a very tight coat in and around their ears which mats quickly. This matted fur can only be removed by cutting it off and it can cause an inflammation if you leave it untreated. Besides a pretty look, grooming also bears a functional component.

A short hint to the common "shearing" which is a disfigurement of the breed in my opinion: In Germany, a lot of people shear their dogs' coats, arguing that the dog wouldn't be so hot. Aussies know how to adapt to changing climates since it's a North American breed. As a result, no shearing is necessary and could in fact be dangerous: Aussies can get a sunburn or skin irritations. In some rare cases, they can even develop metabolism problems or skin diseases.

When Should You Groom?

You will get the best grooming results when you bathe or shower your dog and then dry it with a hair dryer. The coat will be easier to cut and mud and dirt, that may still be in your dog's coat, do not blunt your scissors.

If you want to visit a confirmation show with your dog, I recommend to groom your dog two weeks before the show. This way, a badly cut coat can grow back again and you can hide your mistakes. Shortly before the show starts, you only need to finish up your dog and cut some overlaying hair.

Which Tools Do You Need?

To groom your dog, you will need some tools. If you have to buy them new, you should choose tools with high quality, because you will use them often and nothing is more frustrating than tools that don't do their job or are broken all the time.

Please do not buy brushes from companies that advertise to remove the undercoat. Often they are sold in pet shops. These brushes have a blade at the front that removes the undercoat perfectly, but the blade also cuts off the topcoat. If you use those brushes too often and for too long, you will completely strip down your dog and its coat will be ruined – so please hands off!

Which Brushes Do You Need?

First, I recommend to buy a brush to brush the dog's body. I use a brush called "Hunter Slicker Brush" (the first brush with the orange helve.) I can also recommend a double slicker brush, for example the "Kerbl Premium Care Brush 2 in 1 double" which you can find on the internet to buy. Another brand that I can recommend is Chris Christensen, but it's ultimately your choice. However, the brush should fit into your hand comfortably, the dog should feel comfortable with the tools, and you two should also have fun doing it. The most important thing about the brush is that the bristles are bent at the tip so that you can brush out the undercoat of your Aussie.

While I was looking for a new brush, I ordered all brushes I could find on the internet and I tested with which brush I am most comfortable with and which one delivers the best results. I cannot recommend brushes that have a curved pad. Some brushes are very soft and I guess they are very comfortable for the dog, but you cannot remove a lot of undercoat with them and the bristles bent after the first try. I like the Hunter and Kerbl Brushes most.

Next you need a comb to remove the undercoat and to comb out the tangles in the Aussie's britches. The comb removes the undercoat very effectively without cutting the topcoat, but that can be quite intricate. I always use the brush's side whose bristles are thinly dispersed to get out all of the tangles. I use a normal cheap comb from my local pet store. You can also choose to get a comb of high quality, but a cheap comb without a helve should suffice. I only use the comb during the dog's change of coat and only for a short while. A comb with a handle is more comfortable and prevents pain in your hands when you work longer.

Source of Supply - Brushes	Good to know...
Greyhound Comb	
http://amzn.to/1S1sovV	
Slicker Brushes in different sizes	
http://amzn.to/22i1UeE	

Good to Know: Source of Supply - Brushes

Last but not least, you need a small brush (pin brush) for the paws and hocks (calf bone over the paw on the dog's hind legs). I chose a small square slicker brush, because I do not want to use two brushes. Especially for the paws, you can use a triangular slicker brush, so you can easily brush between the toes. However, for the hocks you need a foursquare brush. I use a small slicker brush from „Land of Dogs", because it is cheaper than the small Hunter Brush, but I can also recommend the Hunter Brush. You should pay attention that this brush is softer than the normal brush for the body.

Which Scissors Do You Need?

You need two scissors, one pair of normal scissors and one pair of thinning scissors. When you buy scissors, you should note that a cheap pair probably won't be of the kind of quality you need and the more expensive the scissors are the better they are. I chose scissors that cost about 30EUR, because 300EUR seemed too expensive for me. I had the pleasure to work with very expensive scissors and I loved it, but unfortunately I don't have a cash cow at home.

You need the trimming scissors to cut the coat under your dog's paw pads, to round the feet, and for the hocks.

The thinning shears allow you to thin out the coat without a straight cut. You can also buy scissors with only one blade with spikes. Ultimately, it's your choice. I chose scissors with both blades spiked. With these scissors you can remove the coat on the paws and you can thin out the fur behind the ears.

To thin out the hair behind the ears you can also use a trim knife. I am not comfortable with trim knives so I use the thinning scissors. The coat under the paw pads can easily be removed with an electric shaver. My experience is that dogs are not comfortable with it and my girls lick their paws more often after having used the razor. I think that the cut hair probably annoys or itches them. That is the reason why I use the trimming shears.

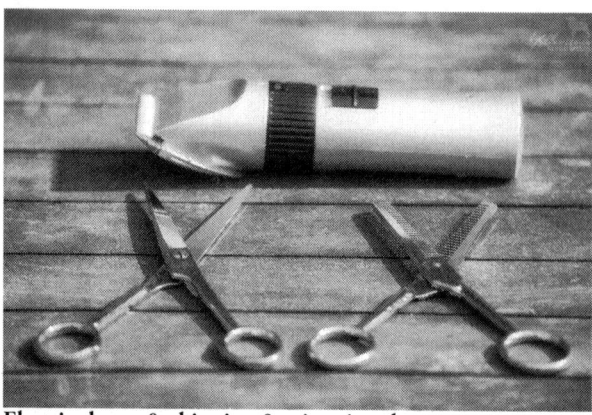

Electric shaver & thinning & trimming shears

Source of Supply - Scissors	Good to know...
Electric Shaver http://amzn.to/1MjT6vo **Thinng & Thrimming shears** http://amzn.to/21sTiPT	

Good to Know: Source of Supply - Scissors

How To Cut The Claws?

To shorten the claws of your dog you have two opportunities.

I use common claw scissors and shorten the claws carefully to not harm the dog. Nevertheless, it happens that I cut off the claw a bit too short and the claw starts to bleed. But no worries. The claw stops to bleed after a while, the dog does hurt a little bit, though. When you cut the claws with claw scissor, the claws become sharp-edged which is why some groomers us a Dremel.

You can buy extensions called wave and a grind tool for the Dremel. With the grind attachment the claws will be honed.

The disadvantage of the Dremel is that it's noisy and a lot of dogs are not comfortable with the feeling on the claws. But the advantage is that any bleeding will stop immediately because of the heat. Furthermore, you can round the claws which looks better.

I had the pleasure to have a breeder grind my dogs' claws with a Dremel. Well, Layla was the only one who let the breeder do it, because I had her in a headlock, so I prefer the claw scissors. It's more fun for me and my dogs with the scissors.

Grooming Table

You can use a grooming table to have a comfortable working height and to provide a safe area from which the dog can't escape. The tables can be foldable, rollable or stationary, and some are adjustable in height if necessary. The top, which is made up of rubber, allows the dog to stand safely. The best size for Aussies is 90x60cm (35 x 23 Inches).

Claw scissor

Source of Supply - Grooming Table	Good to know...
Grooming Table http://amzn.to/1Lo0Txu	

Good to Know: Source of Supply - Grooming Table

Shampoos & Styling Products

A must-have is a shampoo that helps restore the lipid barrier when you wash or bathe your dog. Please do not use shampoo for humans, it harms your dog's skin.

Especially when you prepare your dog for showing, you can use special shampoos that increase your dog's assets or hide mistakes. Shampoos and conditioners are not absolutely necessary, though.

You can use a shampoo that brightens up white or yellowed coat and makes it shine again. I can recommend Chris Christensen's "White on White Shampoo" or „Herbal Whitening Shampoo". The Herbal Shampoo needs to be mixed with water in a ratio of 10:1 or 5:1.

The "White on White Shampoo" spreads white colour molecules on the coat which stay on the coat for 4-6 weeks. In addition to these shampoos, you can buy darkening shampoo which makes black fur shine and highlights the normal coat colour. Chris Christensen's "Black on Black Shampoo" or "Black Opal Shampoo" are wholeheartedly recommended. The "Black Opal Shampoo" should be left on the coat for at least 10 minutes. Then rinse the fur thoroughly.

You can get a shampoo like Chris Christensen's "Red on Red Shampoo" which has the same effect as the "Black on Black Shampoo" only for red dogs. You can mix this shampoo with the black shampoo to match the colour to your dog's coat.

To improve your dog's appearance even further and to perfect your dog's coat, you can also buy a conditioner. Conditioners provide voluminous fur (britches and collar) or straighten the fur (topline). You can use them on both wet or dry fur.

The Chris Christensen "Thick 'n Thicker" adds more volume to the coat and straightens curly or wavy fur. It's available as a spray, foam, gel or mousse and can be used in wet as well as in dry coat. The advantage is that it can be brushed out easily. The coat looks natural and doesn't stick together. This product is highly recommended for dogs who do not have a thick undercoat.

„Puffy Dog" from Plush Puppy also provides a similar effect and can also be used to achieve voluminous fur.

Last but not least, you can use finishing products to improve the fur's gloss, volume, and its moisture. Just try different products on your dog to see which ones you like best. Most companies sell samples of their products, so you can test the products to see which is best for you and your dog.

Source of Supply - Shampoos	Good to know...
Chris Christensen White on White Shampoo	
http://amzn.to/1TKLjyx	
Herbal Whitening Shampoo	
http://bit.ly/1R2iSq4	
Chris Christensen Black on Black Shampoo	
http://amzn.to/1Ud5uFn	
Black Opal Shampoo	
http://bit.ly/1U6W2E0	
Chris Christensen Red on Red Shampoo	
http://amzn.to/1U3EUyS	

Good to Know: Source of Supply - Shampoos

Source of Supply - Conditioner	Good to know...
Chris Christensen Thick N Thicker	
http://amzn.to/1M4laYP	
Puffy Dog	
http://bit.ly/22lsP9j	

Good to Know: Source of Supply - Conditioner

Source of Supply - Finishing Products	Good to know...
PSH Body and Hair Volumen Spray	
http://bit.ly/1QX8Fxq	
PSH X-Treme Shine	
http://bit.ly/1M74f84	
PSH Final Touch	
http://bit.ly/1M74joq	
Shine and Comb	
http://bit.ly/1WpTuOy	
Quick Fix Spray	
http://bit.ly/1U6WEcQ	
Pixie Dust	
http://bit.ly/1R2pXXN	

Good to Know: Source of Supply - Finishing Products

How To Dry Your Dog?

To dry the coat of your dog after bathing it you should use a special dog hair dryer. The dog dryer has more power and can dry the coat faster because of its stronger air blast with which you also reach the undercoat. Besides this, the coat is fluffier after drying and the dog looks as if it had more coat than it actually has.

I use the dryer during my dogs' change of coat to blow all of the dead fur off. This method is often more successful than brushing the fur off and I love doing it. I use a cheap dryer (ca. 70 EUR) that does a very good job, but the handle gets hot after some times. Then the handle will have to cool off before continuing to dry the dog.

Dryers without this weakness cost around 300EUR.

Dog Dryer

Source of Supply - Dog Dryer	Good to know...
Dog Dryer	
http://amzn.to/1Ud6gCj	

Good to Know: Source of Supply - Dog Dryer

Daily Grooming - A Pictured Guide

Brushing the body

1. The following photos of our girl Josie will show you how to brush your dog correctly.

2. Lift your dog onto a grooming table or a regular table to make grooming easy.

3. Start with the body and brush the fur from the front to the back for as long as you get out the undercoat.

Brushing The Body

Brushing The Ears

4. Now focus on the ears. Hold one ear at the tip and lift it up carefully so that you can reach the coat under the ear.

5. Some Aussies have very dense coat under their ears which cannot be brushed easily. Therefore, you should always check the area behind the ears and brush appropriately.

Brushing The Ears

6. If the coat is matted too much, all you can do is cut the tangles with scissors.

Brushing The Toby Collar

7. Next, you should brush the toby collar. To do so, you should grab your dog's muzzle. On the one hand, the dog cannot bite you (useful for when you groom unfamiliar dogs) and on the other hand you can move the head ea-

Brushing The Toby Collar

sily to groom the toby collar.

8. For dogs with a lot of fur (sires for instance), you need to work with a brush with longer slicks, called „undercoat rake", to reach the undercoat.

Brushing The Paws

9. Finally, you brush the paws.

Brushing The paws

On the front legs, Aussies have longer fur which often sticks together with dirt.

That is the reason why you should train your dog to give you its paw. With this trick, the dog helps you with its daily grooming and it enjoys showing you something special.

10. On the pictures, you can see that Josie knows this procedure and is very relaxed and calm.

Brushing The Britches

11. If you are satisfied with the dog's look at the front, you should focus on the rear side.

First, you start to groom the britches of your Aussie. You grab the dog by the belly to prevent the dog from sitting down and to support it at the same time.

12. Brush the sides of your dog's tails (or where the tail should be if you have an NBT or docked Aussie). Do not worry, you will not touch or hurt the genitals, because the dog covers it with its tail. With NBT or docked dogs you should be a little bit more careful.

Brushing The Britches

Brushing The Tail

13. Last but not least you should brush your dog's tail, so that the tail will swing nicely when the dog moves.

14. Grab the tail and pull the brush from the bottom to the tip of the tail. Use your dog's opposition reflex for this task. The dog will lean forward automatically when you pull the brush to the tail's end.

Brushing The Tail From Above

15. Repeat this step the same way also on the upper side.

Brushing The Tail

Positive Reinforcement

16. Do not forget to reward your dog and praise it a lot.

17. You should treat your dog after every grooming session. This way you boost calm behaviour and the relationship between you two becomes stronger.

Treats After Grooming

Cutting The Claws

The dog's claws continuously grow - just like human nails. Normally, the claws shorten by themselves when walking on hard floors.

Sometimes, the claws need to be shortened. You can use special claw scissors which work similarly to our human nail scissors: You place the part of the claw that you want to cut off between the blades and push the handles together to cut off the claw.

> **Claws Supplied with Blood** *Good to know...*
>
> The claw consists of a part that is supplied with blood and one part that is not supplied with blood.
>
> When your dog has bright claws, you can recognise a pink and a white part.
>
> The white part is dead and can be cut off. Be careful not to shorten the claws too much.
>
> Humans also hurt when they shorten their nails too much. Naturally, dogs also hurt when their claws are too short!

Good to Know: Claws Supplied with Blood

Pay attention that you do not cut into the pink part of the claw. Otherwise, the claw will start to bleed and your dog probably won't give you its paws voluntarily next time. If you do not trust yourself to cut the dog's claws, you can also ask a vet to help you.

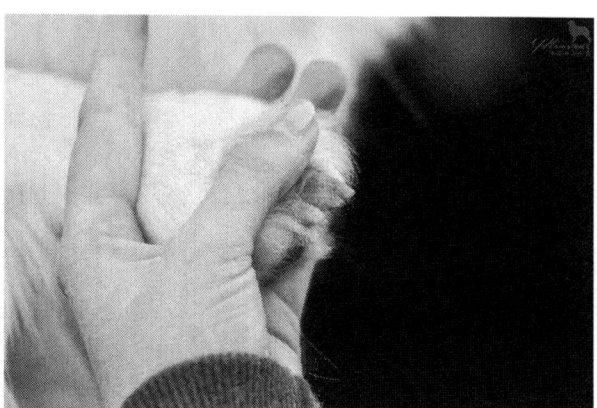

In Germany, shortening the claws costs around 8 **Uncut Claw**
EUR. Another option would be to let your breeder show you how to cut the claws. But let's be honest, you also wouldn't go to the doctor to get your nails cut, would you? Just try it and do not be scared: Cut off small parts first, so that you cannot hurt your dog and so that it does not associate getting its claws cut with pain.

After cutting, you can praise your dog for good behaviour.

Claw Cutting Guide

18. On the following photo, you can see two of the four front claws of an Aussie. Note that the front part is white („dead") and the hind part – not easy to see - is the pink („alive") part. You can see that the claw is angular to the bottom.

If you cut the claw, only cut the white part not the pink part. It's better to cut off only a little bit at a time than to risk harming your dog and to risk that the claw starts bleeding which may result in your dog being anxious and developing phobias.

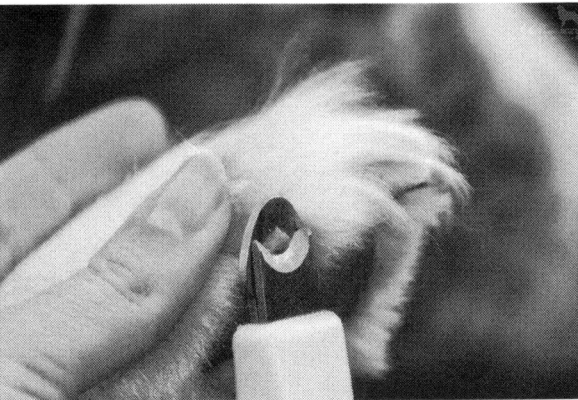

19. The claws are usually a little bit rough after cutting and the dog will have to smoothen them again by running. You do not need to cut the claws on the hind legs of your dog, because the dog will shorten them by itself while running on hard floors.

Cutting The Claw

20. The so called dewclaw, which is located on the inner side of your dog's front legs (sometimes also at the hind legs), should also always be checked. This claw should not become too long, otherwise it can grow in.

Positive Reinforcement

21. Last but not least, do not forget to praise your dog.

22. You should reward your dog after every grooming session to boost calm behaviour and improve the relationship between you two.

Treats After Cutting The Claw

Show Grooming - A Pictured Guide

Removing The Fur Under The Paws

23. Lift your dog onto a table and make sure that it cannot jump off the table.

24. Now, stand next to your dog and grab the front paw closest to you with your left hand. Grab the paw and bend it so that you can see the bottom. Hold the paw tightly as if you were shoeing a horse.

25. Then, cut all the fur between the paw pads with your trimming scissors until you can see all the toes well enough.

Attention:

Cut carefully! Dogs, that are not familiar with grooming, are ticklish and can kick with both front and hind legs. Be careful not to hurt yourself or your dog!

Removing The Fur Under The Paw

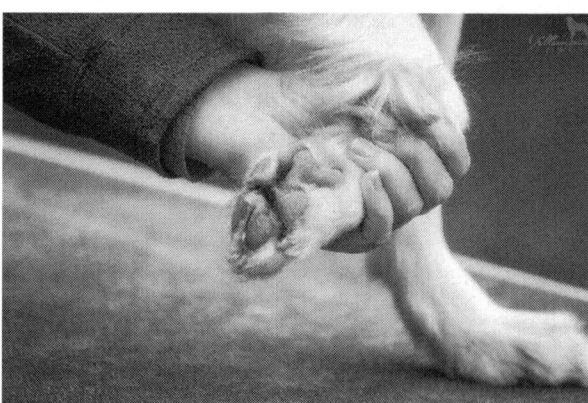
Groomed Front Paw

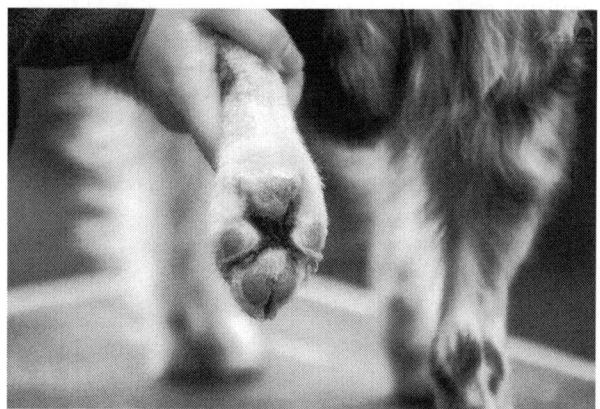
Groomed Back Paw

Removing The Fur on The Paws

26. Position yourself in front of the dog. Start with the left front paw and place it in your hand or make the dog give you its paw.

27. It's best you hold the paw with your index finger and your thumb at the thenar eminence.

28. Hold the paw tightly at the joint and use the small or triangular slicker brush to brush the hair between the toes up. Some dogs pull back their paw, because they are not used to getting their paws brushed which is why you need to hold it tightly and pull the paw back to you.

29. Then take the thinning scissors and cut the lifted fur to round the paw.

30. Brush the rest of the fur down and evaluate your result. Repeat the procedure when some of the fur still sticks out.

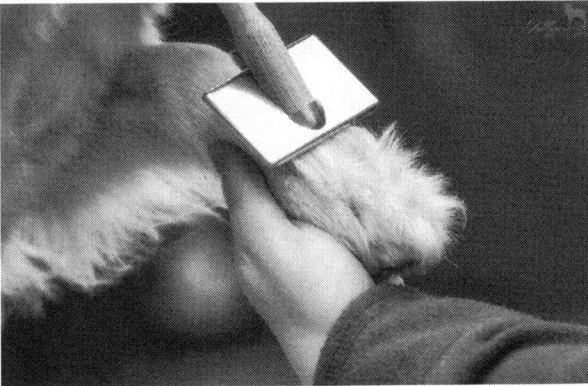

Brush The Hair Up

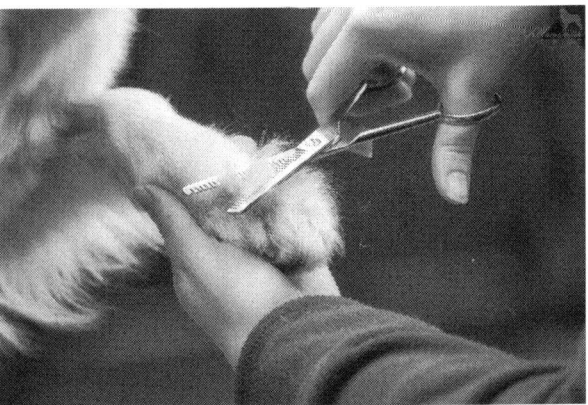

Round The Paw

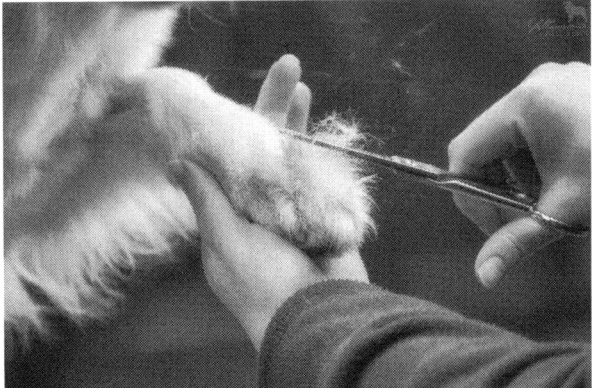

Shorten The Fur

Cutting The Fur on The Back of The Front Paws

31. Position yourself next to your dog again and work on the paw beside you. Grab the paw from the front and feel the thenar eminence.

32. Put your middle finger under the thenar and hold the paw tightly.

33. Remove all the fur between the thenar and the paw with your thinning scissors.

34. You can cut from the side and from above, but be careful not to cut holes in the fur.

35. The paws and the feather fur should be accentuated when you are done.

36. Last but not least, you can cut off off-standing fur on the paw with your trimming shears to accentuate the round paw.

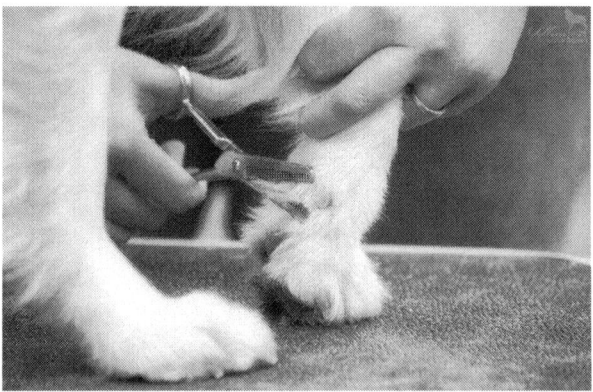

Removing The Hair at The Rear Side of The Foot

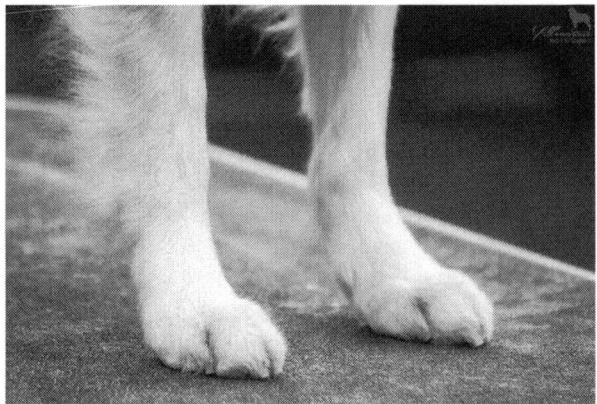

Groomed Front Paws

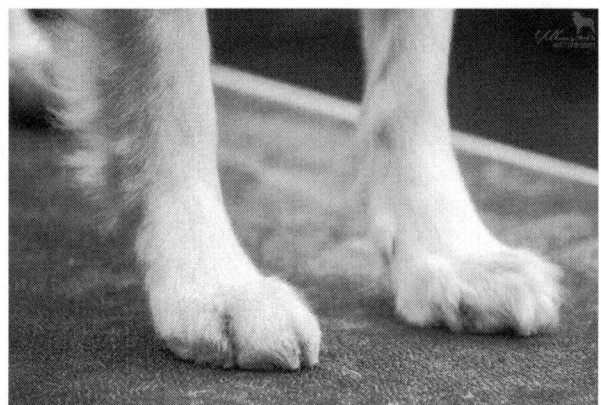

Comparision: Groomed and Ungroomed Front Paws

Grooming Hind Paws

37. Position yourself behind your dog and lift up one hind paw. Grab the hocks from between the hind legs. Cut off all of the fur that is between the toes with your trimming shears as you have read it in the chapter „Removing The Fur on The Paws ".

Groomed Hint Paw

38. Next, position yourself next to the dog and grab a hind paw by the hocks from between the back legs and lift the paw. This way, your dog can stand comfortably on your hand. Now, brush the fur up with a slicker brush.

39. With your thinning shears, you now cut of all the off-standing fur and round the paw with your trimming shears while the paw rests back on the table.

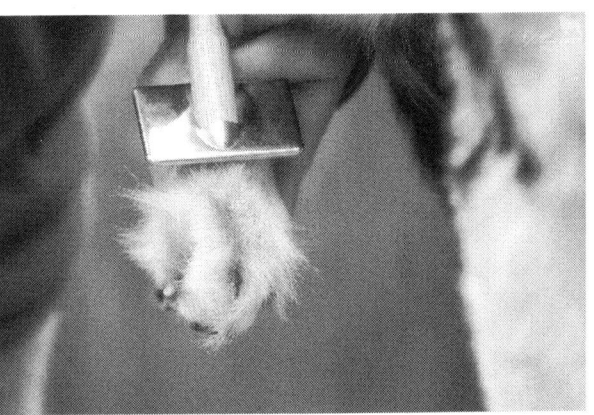

Brushing The Fur up

40. Brush down the rest of the fur.

41. Now and then, you should position the two paws next to each other to check and compare their looks.

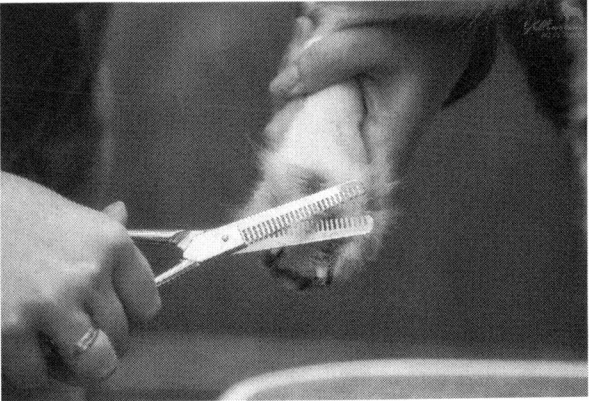

Rounding The Paw

Grooming The Hocks

42. Position yourself behind your dog and place both hind legs in parallel. Grab around the hocks with both hands and pull the hind legs carefully to the table edge.

43. Give your dog the command to stand calmly and be careful so that your dog doesn't fall off the table.

44. A second person can help you to hold the dog in place and to pay attention to the dog so it does not fall off the table and hurts itself.

45. When you positioned both paws orthogonally to the table edge, you can start to brush the fur on the hocks up with your small slicker brush. Grab the hocks with your left hand. Your arm secures the other paw, so that you dog steps on your arm when he moves. Usually, the fur is a little bit dense and needs to be treated a bit more thoroughly.

46. Grab the hocks with your left hand and push the standing-off hair with your thumb and thenar to the right side, so that they stick out.

47. Cut off all the off-standing fur with your trimming shears in a downward motion.

Position on The Table

Brushing The Fur up

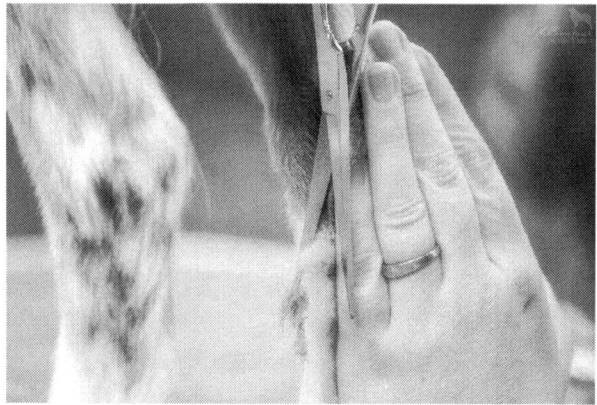
Cut on The Left

48. Next, you brush all the fur to the left side and you put your left hand flat on the hocks to push the hair to the left.
49. Again, cut off the fur.
50. Brush the leftover hair down.

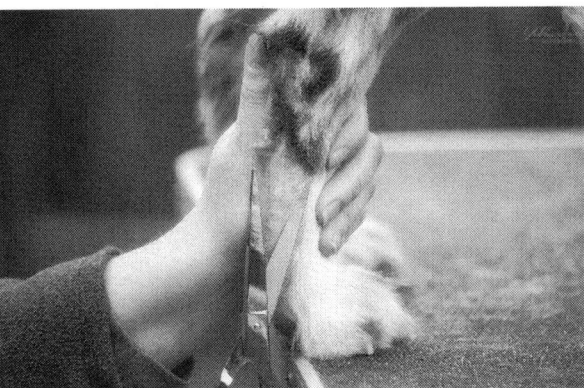

Cutting on The Right

Hind legs need to be orthogonal to the table edge

Grooming The Ears

51. Positon yourself next to your dog and lift up one ear at the tip by grabbing it with your index finger and thumb. Bend the ear back so that you can see the inside of the ear.

52. Hold the ear and pull tight and start shortening the fur with your thinning shears.

    Attention: There is a little lobe on the lower side of the ear. Please be careful not to cut it.

53. Round the ear and check your work every now and then by looking at your dog from the front. It's best to only take off little by little. It's easy to cut off more than putting some fur back on.

54. Shorten all the fur that grows out of the ears. Rose Ears are more difficult to cut than button ears.

55. Next, you need to shorten the fur behind the ears. Grab the ear at the tip with your index finger and thumb again, but this time pull the ear to the front. You can put your hand on the dog's muzzle so you can prevent the dog from moving its head to you.

56. Now, shorten all the fur behind the ears with your thinning shears.

57. Check your cut from time to time and look at your dog from the front.

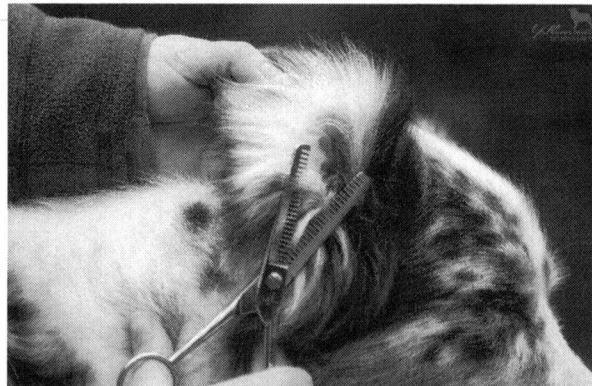
Grab The Ear at The Tip

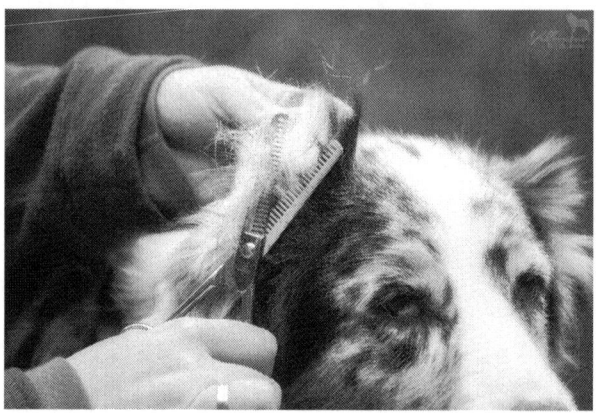
Shorten The Hair in The Ear

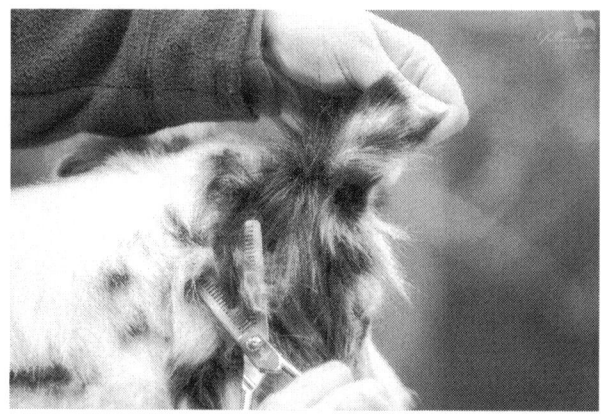
Shorten The Hair Behind the Ear

58. Often, you can shorten the fur under the ears with a trim knife or with your thinning shears. If you use the scissors, then cut upwards and parallel to the head.

59. Shorten all the fur overlapping the ear.

60. Finally, you can cut the outline of the ear with your trimming shears. You need a very calm hand to do so and your dog needs and a lot of practice.

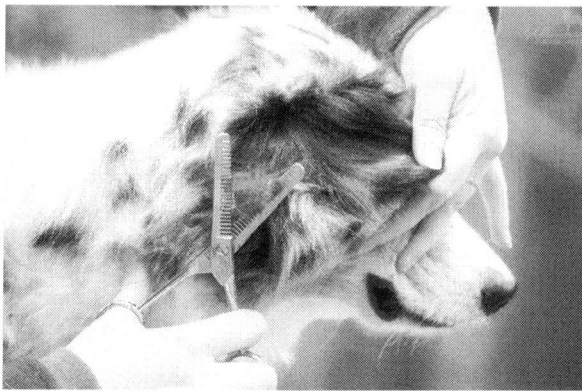

Grabbing The Ear

Summary

Congratulations, now you know how to groom your dog no matter if it's a pet dog or you want to prepare your dog for showing.

I hope that the photos help you while grooming your dog. Now, you should practise and improve your techniques and it will be easier to style your dog someday.

If you have questions or helpful suggestions, then you can write me an email: info@yellowstoneaussies.de.

Ungroomed Ears

Groomed Left Ear, Ungroomed Right Ear

Groomed Aussie

Table of Figures

Brushing The Body 15
Brushing The Britches 16
Brushing The Ears 15
Brushing The Fur up 23
Brushing The paws 16
Brushing The Tail 17
Brushing The Tail From Above 17
Brushing The Toby Collar 15
Brush The Hair Up 21
Comparision: Groomed and Ungroomed Front Paws 22
Cut on The Left 24
Cutting The Claw... 19
Dog Dryer.. 14
Electric shaver & thinning & trimming shears 10
Grabbing The Ear.. 27
Grab The Ear at The Tip.. 26
Groomed Aussie 28
Groomed Back Paw... 20
Groomed Front Paw... 20
Groomed Front Paws... 22
Groomed Hint Paw 23
Groomed Left Ear, Ungroomed Right Ear... 28
Hind legs need to be orthogonal to the table edge 25
Our Yellowstone Pack Josie, Maisy, Layla & Seven 5
Position on The Table.. 24
Removing The Fur Under The Paw 20
Rounding The Paw... 23
Round The Paw.. 21
Shorten The Fur 21
Shorten The Hair Behind the Ear.. 26
Shorten The Hair in The Ear 26
The author & some of her dogs Layla, Maisy & Josie 5
Treats After Cutting The Claw... 19
Treats After Grooming 17
Uncut Claw.. 18
Ungroomed Ears 28

Good to Know

Good to Know: Claws Supplied with Blood 18
Good to Know: Source of Supply - Brushes 9
Good to Know: Source of Supply - Conditioner 13
Good to Know: Source of Supply - Dog Dryer 14
Good to Know: Source of Supply - Finishing Products 13
Good to Know: Source of Supply - Grooming Table 11
Good to Know: Source of Supply - Scissors 10
Good to Know: Source of Supply - Shampoos 12

Made in the USA
Monee, IL
12 April 2021